# Contents

Amazing Paintings    page 2

Cool Cat and the Cave    page 12

Diana Bentley
and Sylvia Karavis

Story illustrated by
Andrés Martinez

# Before Reading

## Find out about

- Some Stone Age cave paintings

## Tricky words

- cave
- walls
- paintings
- found
- showed
- people
- famous

Introduce these tricky words and help the reader when they come across them later!

## Text starter

In France in 1940 some boys made a great discovery. They found a cave. They went into the cave and saw paintings made by Stone Age cave people.

# Amazing Paintings

The boys went into the cave.

They looked at the walls.
They saw lots of paintings.

# The paintings looked very old.

The paintings were 20,000 years old.

The boys went on and found more caves.

They went into the caves and looked at the walls.

On the walls were more paintings.

The paintings were made by cave people.

The paintings were made in the Stone Age.

The boys showed people
the caves and the very old
paintings on the walls.

The boys were famous.

They had found the best
cave paintings in the world.

# Quiz

## Text Detective

- Who had painted the pictures on the cave walls?
- Would you have gone into the caves?

## Word Detective

- **Phonic Focus:** Initial letter sounds

  Page 6: Find a word beginning with the phoneme 'w'.
- Page 7: Find a word made from two small words.
- Page 10: Find a word meaning 'well-known'.

## Super Speller

Read these words:

by    had    in

Now try to spell them!

HA! HA! HA!

**Q** How can you walk through walls?

**A** Use the door!

11

# Before Reading

## In this story

 Cool Cat

 The children

## Tricky words

- children
- can't
- out
- hurray
- stay
- lighthouse
- whoops

Introduce these tricky words and help the reader when they come across them later!

## Story starter

When Cat hears a cry for help he turns into Cool Cat. One day, Cat was sleeping on the beach. Then he heard some children shouting for help.

# Cool Cat and the Cave

"Help!" said the children.
"We can't get out."

"This is a job for Cool Cat," said Cat.
"I will get the children out."

The children saw Cool Cat.

"Hurray for Cool Cat,"
said the children.
"Cool Cat will get us out."

"Get on my back,"
said Cool Cat.
"I will get you out."

The children sat on Cool Cat's back.

"Stay cool," said Cool Cat.

"Hurray!" said the children.
"Cool Cat got us out."

Then the children saw the lighthouse.

"Help! Help!" said the children.
"We can't get back!"

"Whoops!" said Cool Cat.

# Quiz

## Text Detective

- How did Cool Cat rescue the children?
- Was Cool Cat really cool?

## Word Detective

- **Phonic Focus:** Initial letter sounds

  Page 18: Find a word beginning with the phoneme 's'.
- Page 14: Find two small words in 'this'.
- Page 22: Find the word that means 'cannot'.

## Super Speller

Read these words:

# we    saw    sat

Now try to spell them!

**HA! HA! HA!**

**Q** What happened to the cat who swallowed a ball of wool?

**A** She had mittens.

24